Written by Elsie Guerrero
Illustrated by Tullip Studio

Copyright © 2025 Elsie Publishing Company. DBA Promote Inclusion Books.

Washington, D.C. All rights reserved.

No part of this publication may be reproduced, distributed, or transmitted in any form or by any means, including photocopying, recording, or other electronic or mechanical methods, without the prior written permission of the publisher, except in the case of brief quotations embodied in critical reviews and certain other noncommercial uses permitted by copyright laws of the United States of America.

ISBN: 979-8-9923027-9-0

A is for Addison's Disease and Alzheimer's Disease.

Addison's disease happens when the adrenal glands' fail to produce sufficient amounts of the hormones cortisol and aldosterone. This can make someone feel very tired, weak, or sick.

Alzheimer's disease is a condition that usually impacts older people. They have trouble remembering and doing things that they would naturally do independently.

B is for Bowen Disease and Bell's Palsy.

Bowen disease is like a little patch on the skin that doesn't heal correctly. It might look red, rough, or a bit scaly, kind of like a dry spot. It happens when some tiny skin cells don't grow the right way.

Bell's palsy is a condition that causes sudden weakness or paralysis of the muscles on one side of the face.

C is for Congenital Heart Disease, Crohn's Disease, and Cystic Fibrosis.

Congenital heart disease occurs when a baby is born with an abnormal heart. The heart may have an extra hole or a part that's too small or too big.

Crohn's disease is a chronic, inflammatory condition of the digestive tract.

Cystic fibrosis is a genetic disorder that affects the lungs, digestive system, and other organs.

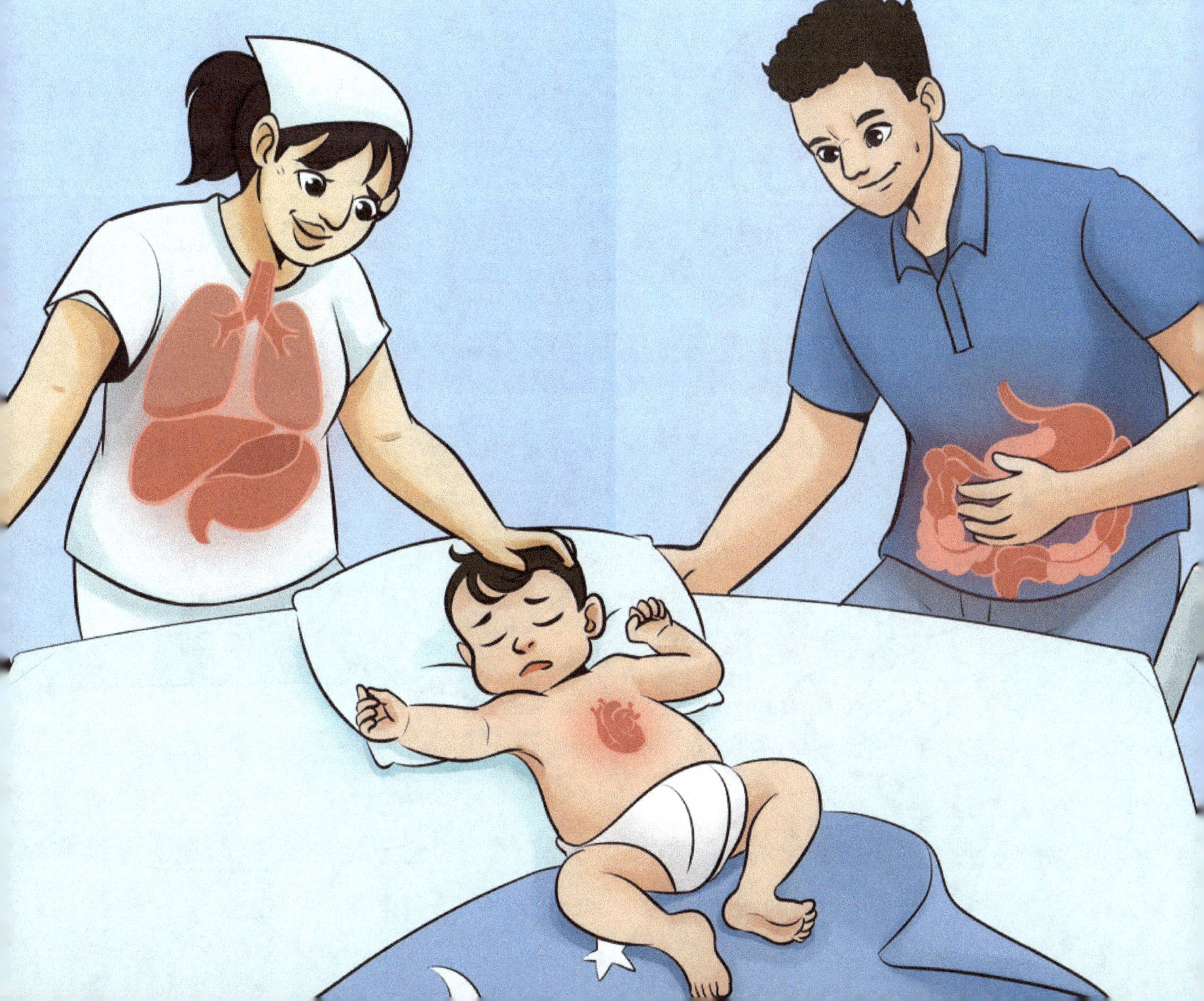

D is for Diverticulosis Disease.

Diverticulosis is a condition where small pouches form in the wall of the colon. Most of the time, they don't cause any problems. But if food or germs get stuck in them, they can get swollen and make someone's tummy hurt a lot.

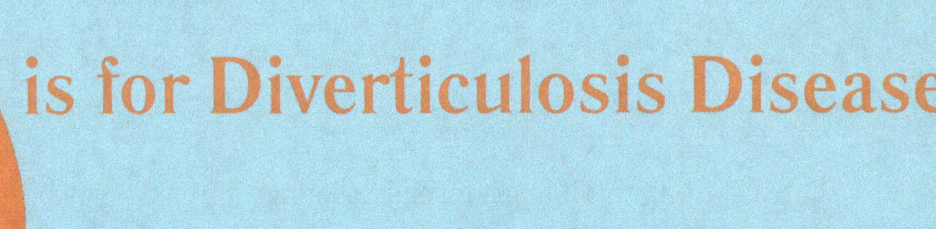

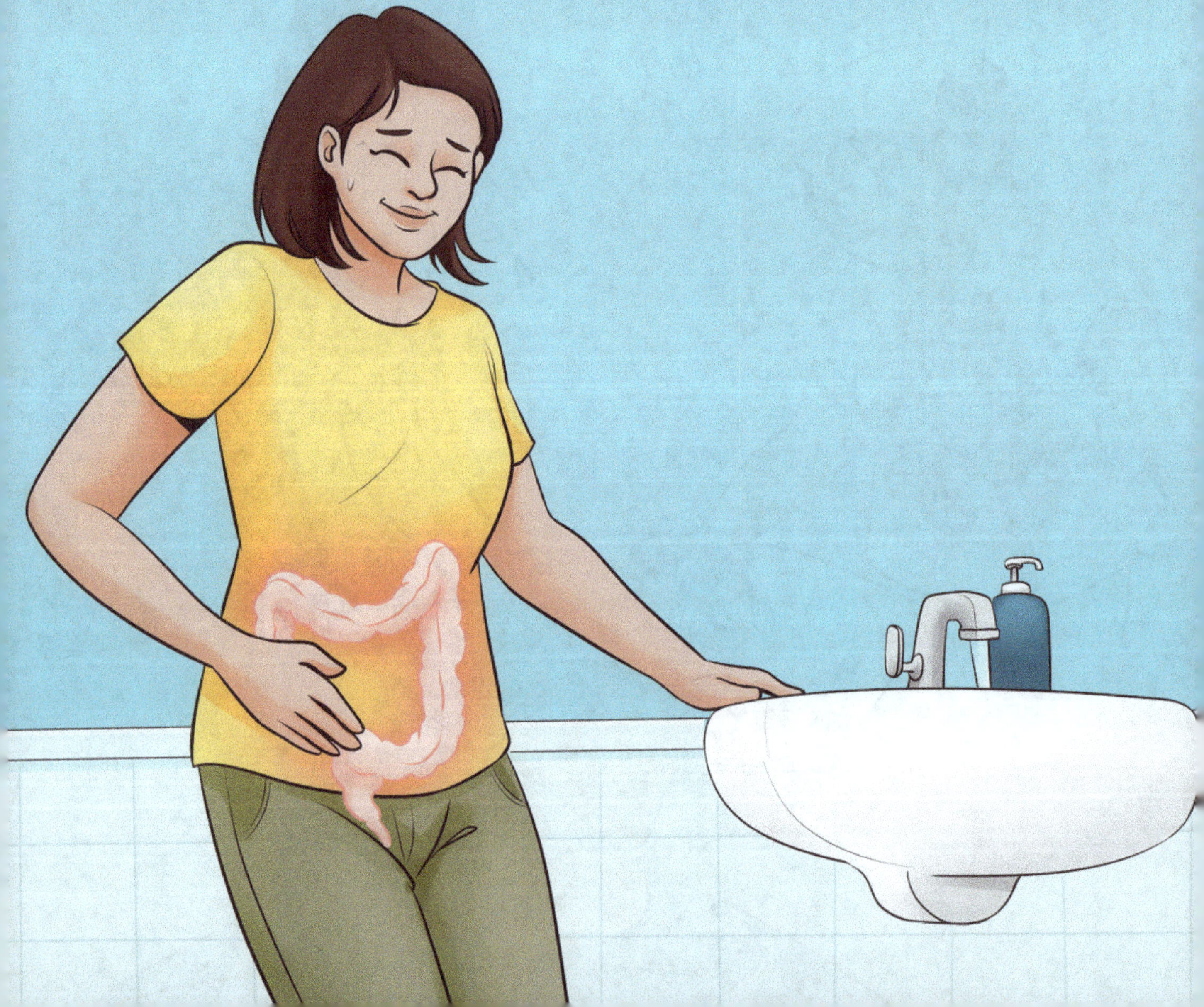

E is for Ebola Virus Disease.

Ebola is a sickness caused by a virus, which can cause severe symptoms including fever, diarrhea, muscle pain, skin rash, and tiredness. The virus spreads when people touch someone who is already infected.

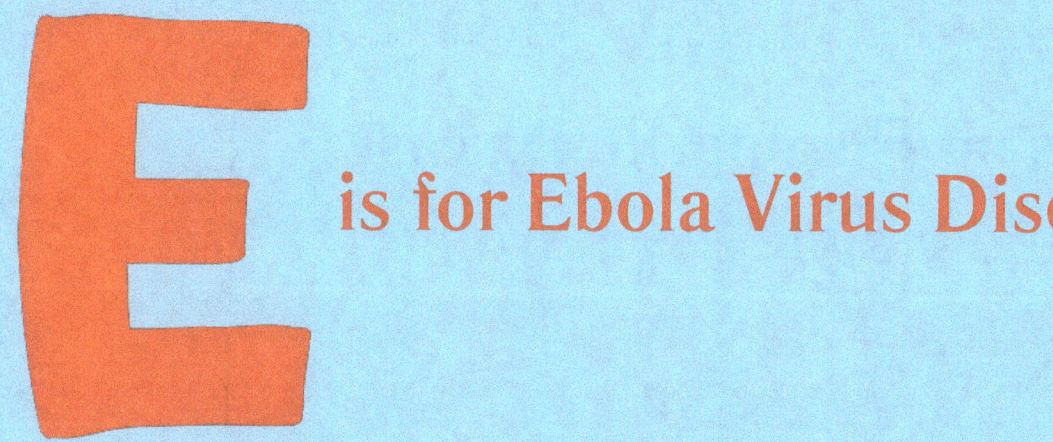

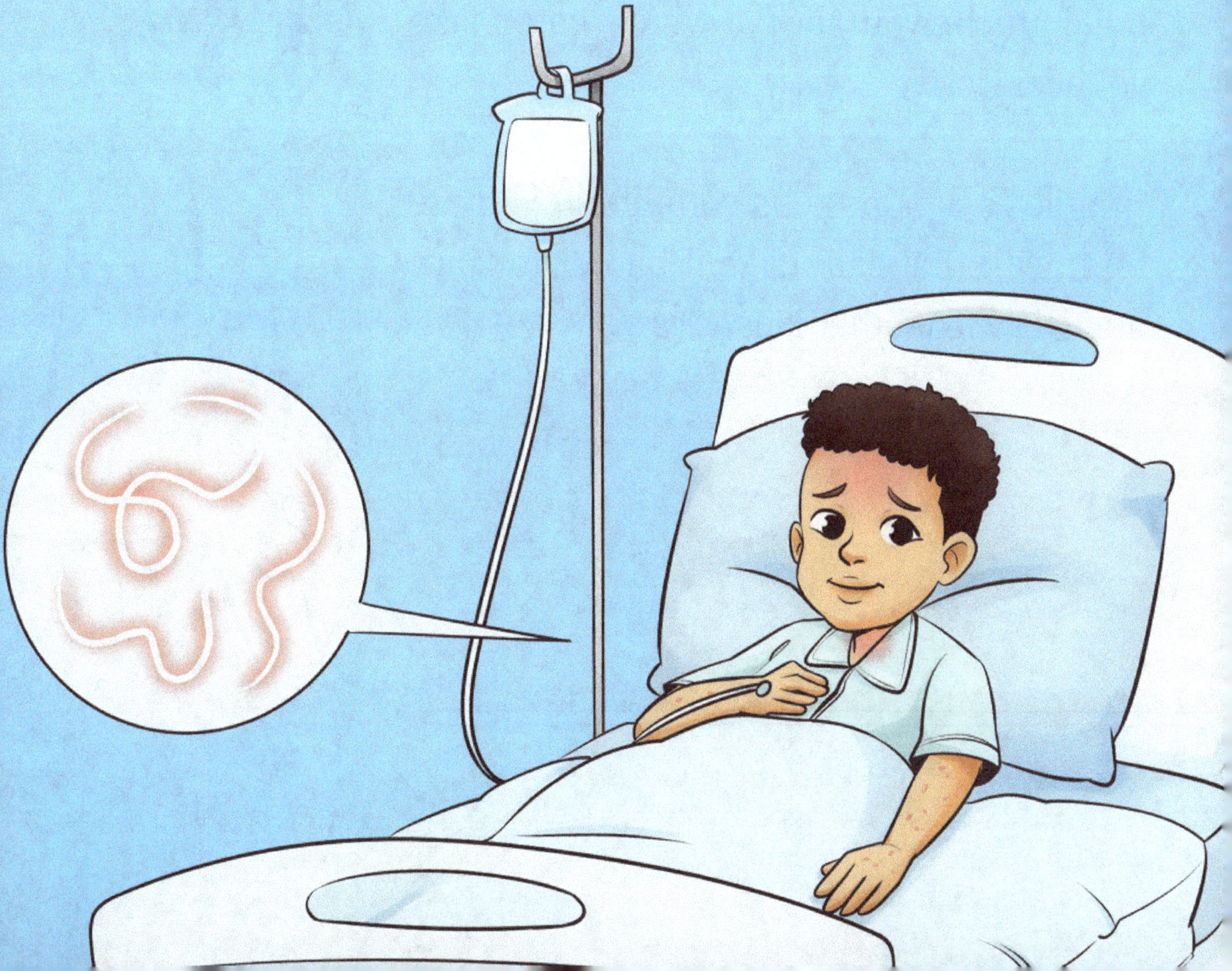

F is for Ferroportin Disease and Fragile X Syndrome.

Ferroportin disease is a rare sickness you are born with. It makes too much iron build up in your body, which can make you feel sick.

Fragile X Syndrome is something you are born with that can make it harder to learn and grow like other kids.

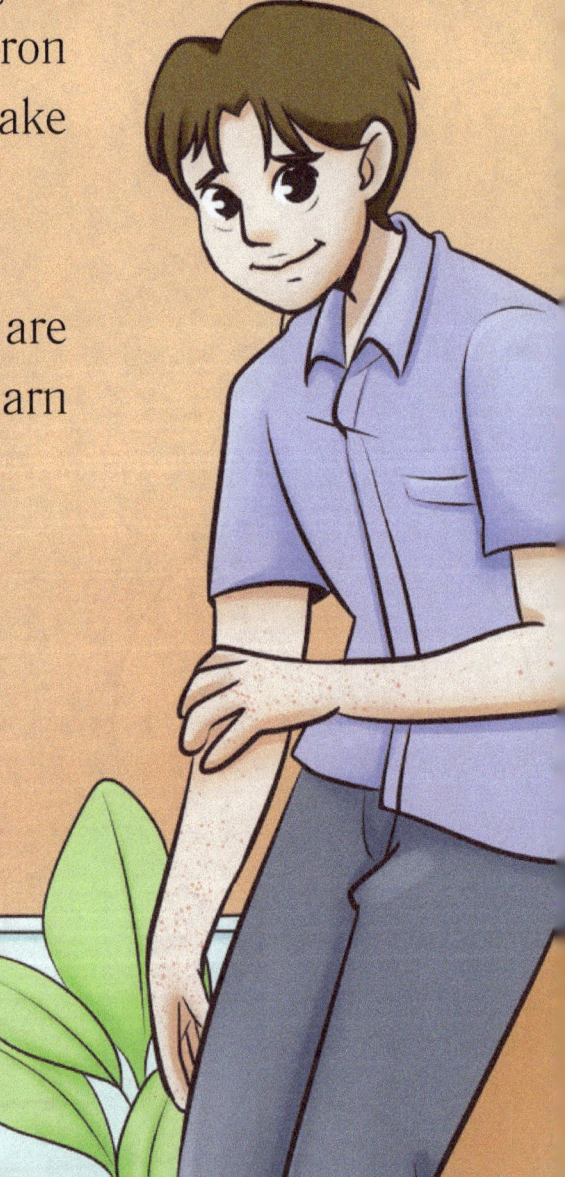

G is for Gastroesophageal Reflux Disease and Gum Disease.

Gastroesophageal reflux disease is when stomach acid flows back up into the food pipe causing a burning feeling in the chest or a sour taste in the mouth. It happens because the muscle that keeps food in the stomach doesn't close correctly.

Gum disease is an infection of the gums that can make them red, swollen, and bleed.

H is for **Huntington's Disease** and **Hypnic Jerks.**

Huntington's disease is a condition that affects the brain, making it harder to control movements, think clearly, and manage emotions over time.

Hypnic jerks occurs when a person is asleep and the muscle involuntary twitches.

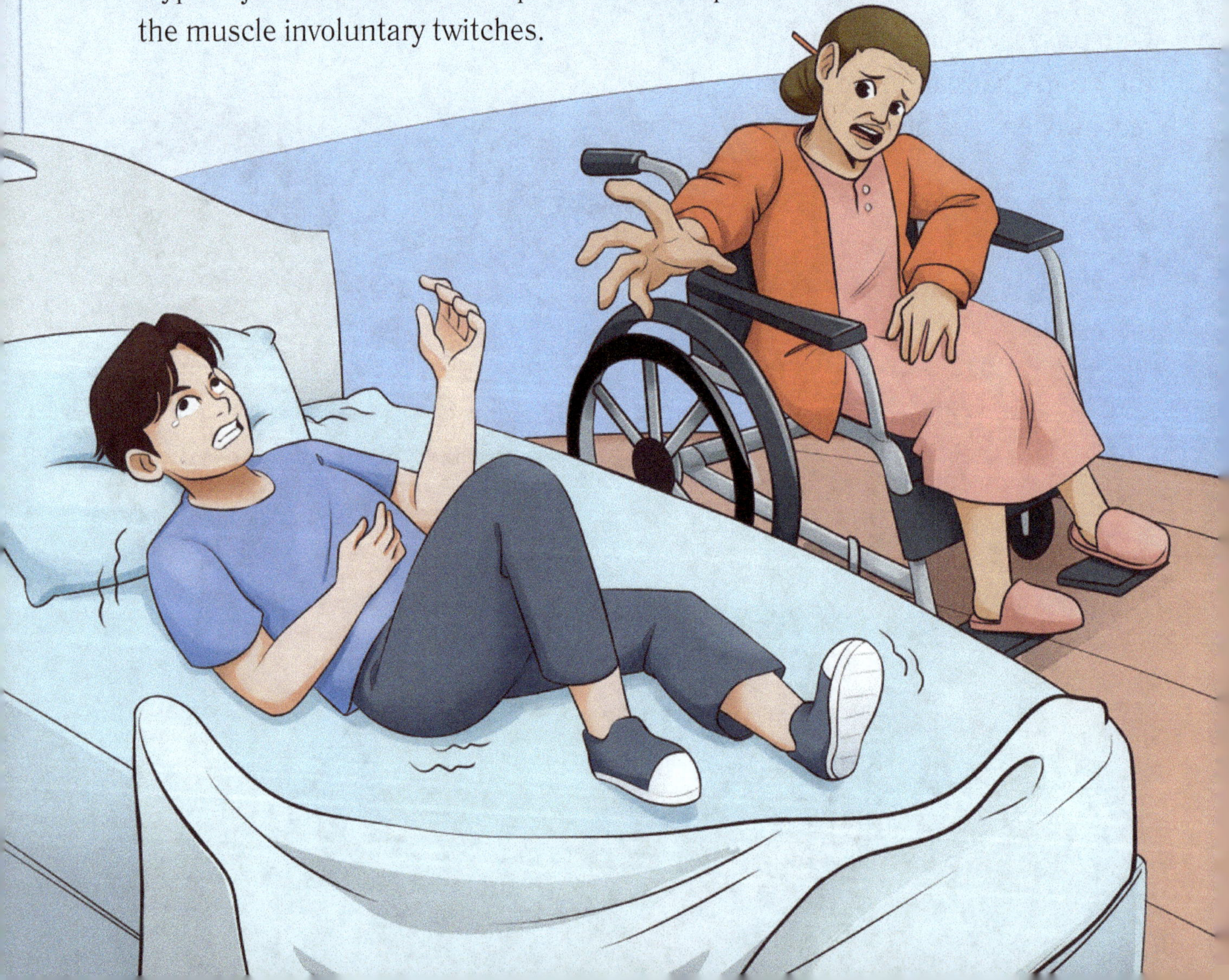

I is for Immune Thrombocytopenia and Ivemark Syndrome.

Immune thrombocytopenia is when the body's immune system gets confused and starts attacking its platelets, which are the tiny cells that help stop the bleeding from cuts or bruises. When there are not enough platelets, a person can bruise easily, have nosebleeds, or bleed longer from minor cuts.

Ivemark Syndrome is a rare congenital disorder where a person is born without a spleen and has abnormalities in how their organs develop, especially the heart and major blood vessels.

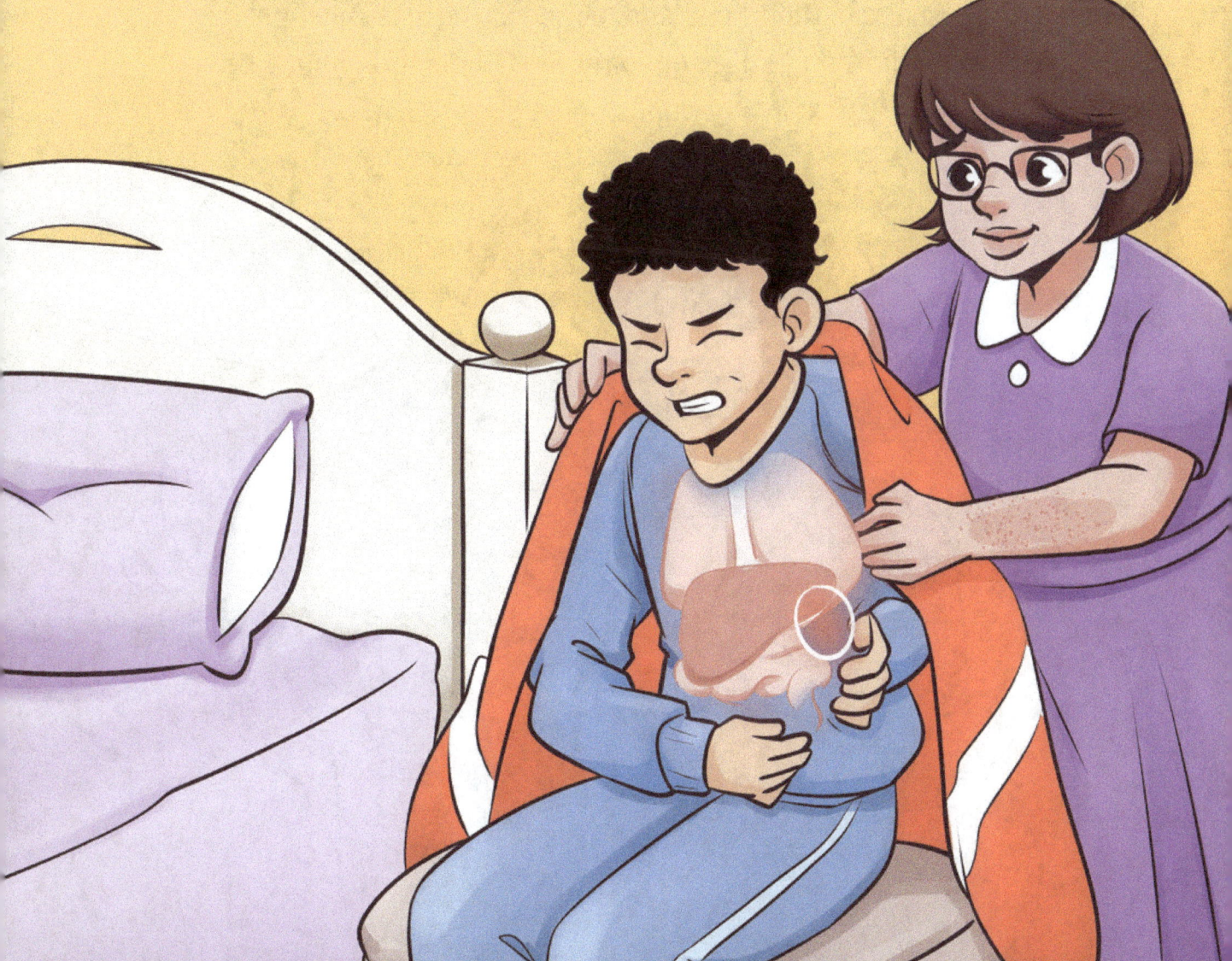

J is for Joubert Syndrome and Jackson-Weiss Syndrome.

Joubert Syndrome is a rare genetic disorder that affects brain development, which controls balance and coordination. It can also impact breathing, eye movements, muscle tone, and sometimes intellectual development.

Jackson-Weiss Syndrome is a condition where a baby is born with changes in the shape of their head and feet because the bones grow differently. Their skull may fuse too early, and their toes might be unusually shaped or stuck in a bent position.

K is for Kidney Disease.

Kidney disease is a condition where the kidneys are damaged and can no longer filter blood as effectively as they should. The kidneys help remove waste, excess fluids, and balance minerals in the body, so when they aren't working correctly, waste can build up and lead to serious health problems.

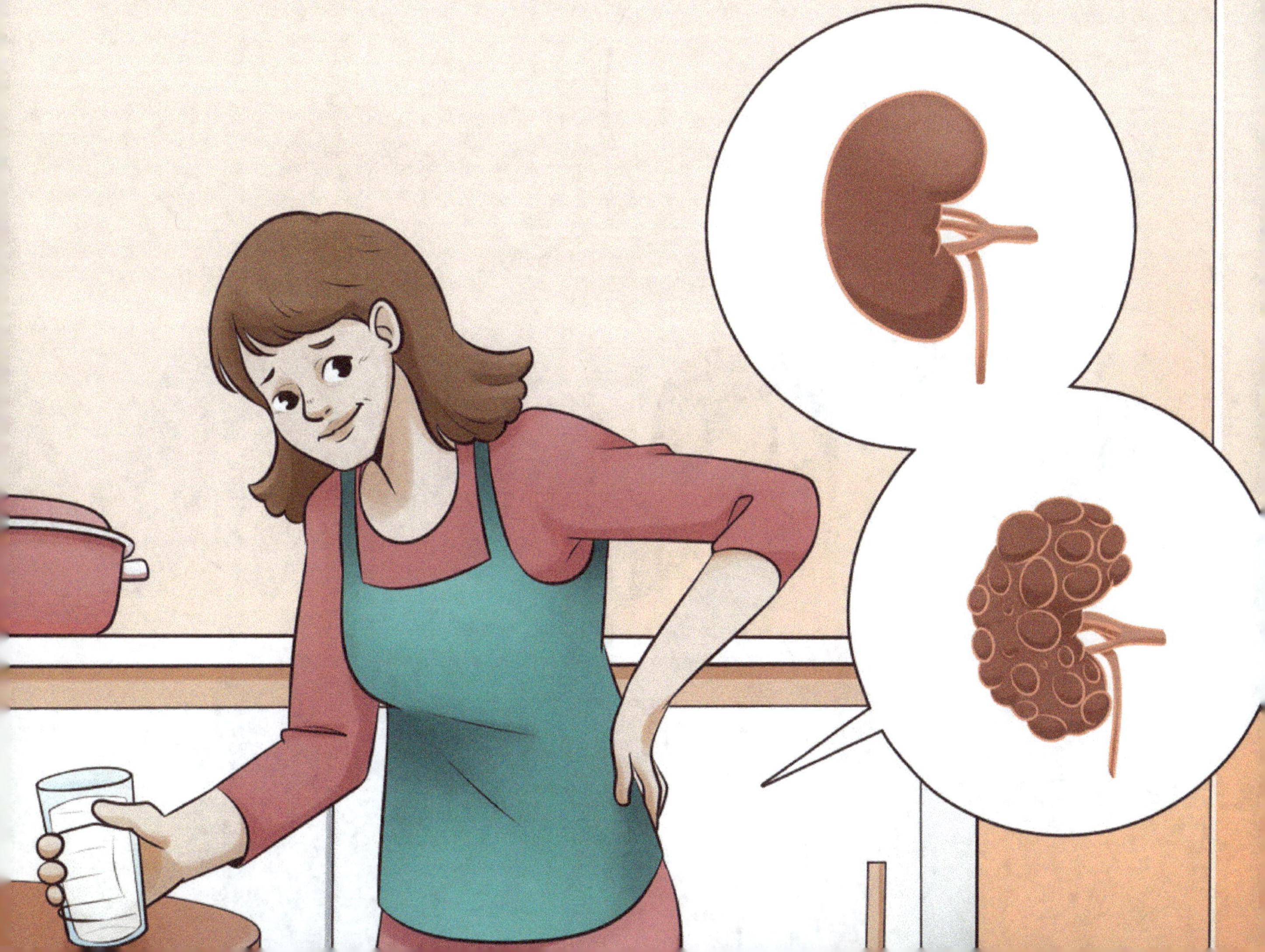

L is for Liver Disease and Lyme Disease.

Liver disease means something is wrong with the liver, which is a vital part of the body. The liver helps your body use food, get rid of harmful stuff, make something called bile to help with digestion, and store energy. When the liver is injured or becomes ill, it can cause other health problems.

Lyme disease is a sickness you can get from the bite of a tiny bug called a tick. The tick has harmful germs inside it that can make you feel sick.

M is for Meniere's Disease and Motor Neurone Disease.

Meniere's disease is a disorder of the inner ear that affects hearing and balance. It causes a spinning sensation, ringing in the ears, hearing loss, and a feeling of fullness or pressure in the ear.

Motor neurone disease happens when the brain and spinal cord's nerve cells that control muscles stop working correctly. Over time, it becomes harder to move, talk, swallow, or even breathe. The muscles weaken because the brain can no longer send messages to them.

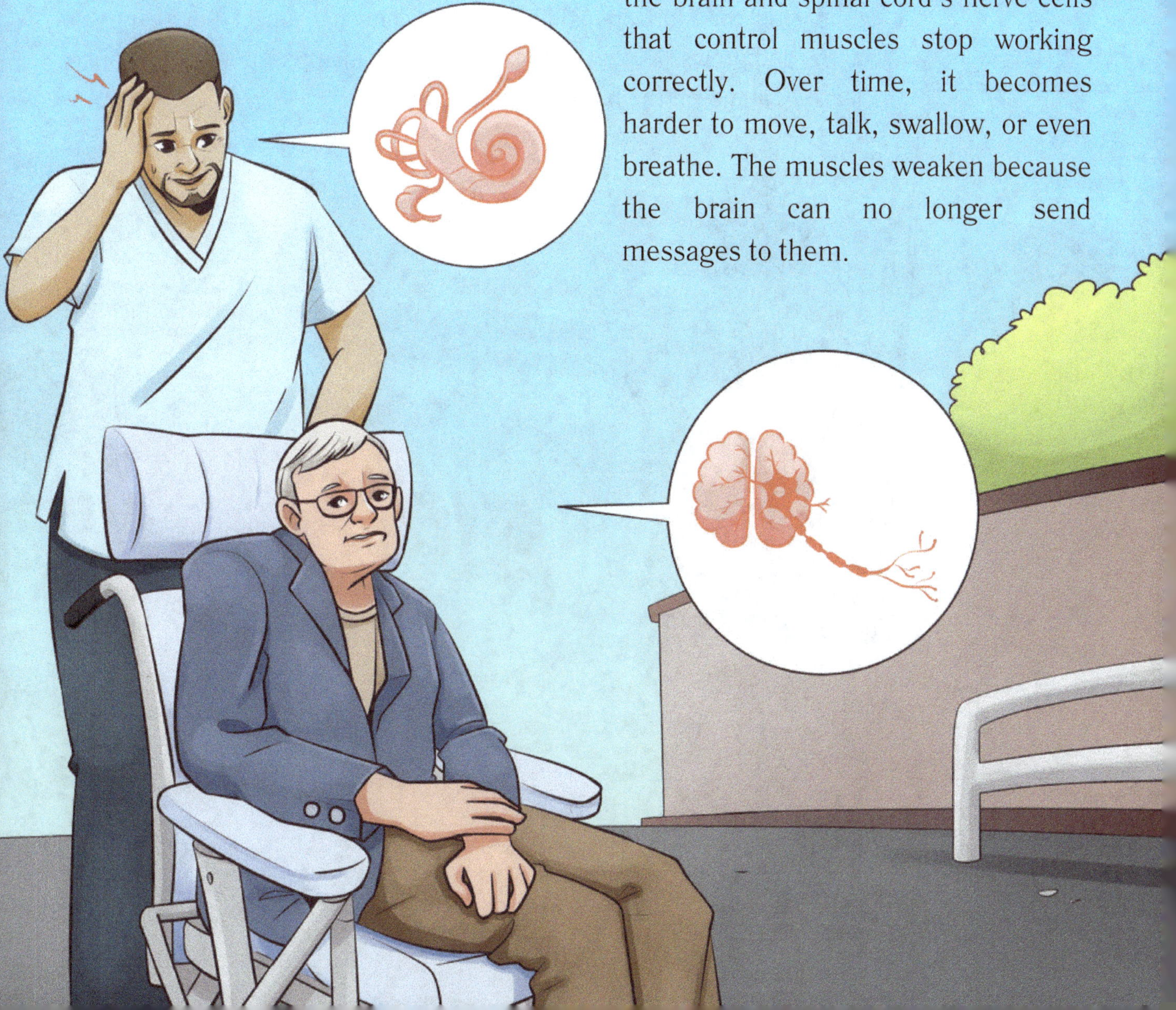

 **is for Non-alcoholic Fatty Liver Disease and Neurofibromatosis.**

Non-alcoholic fatty liver disease happens when there's too much fat in the liver, even though you don't drink too much alcohol. Over time, this extra fat can cause swelling and damage the liver, and it can lead to more serious health issues.

Neurofibromatosis (NF) is a condition that causes tumors to grow on nerves in or outside your body. Everyone experiences NF differently, and there are two types. NF type 1 can lead to spots or bumps that may appear on the skin or inside the body, and can affect how a person learns and grows. NF2 can lead to tumors, causing issues with balance, hearing, and even the brain or spinal cord.

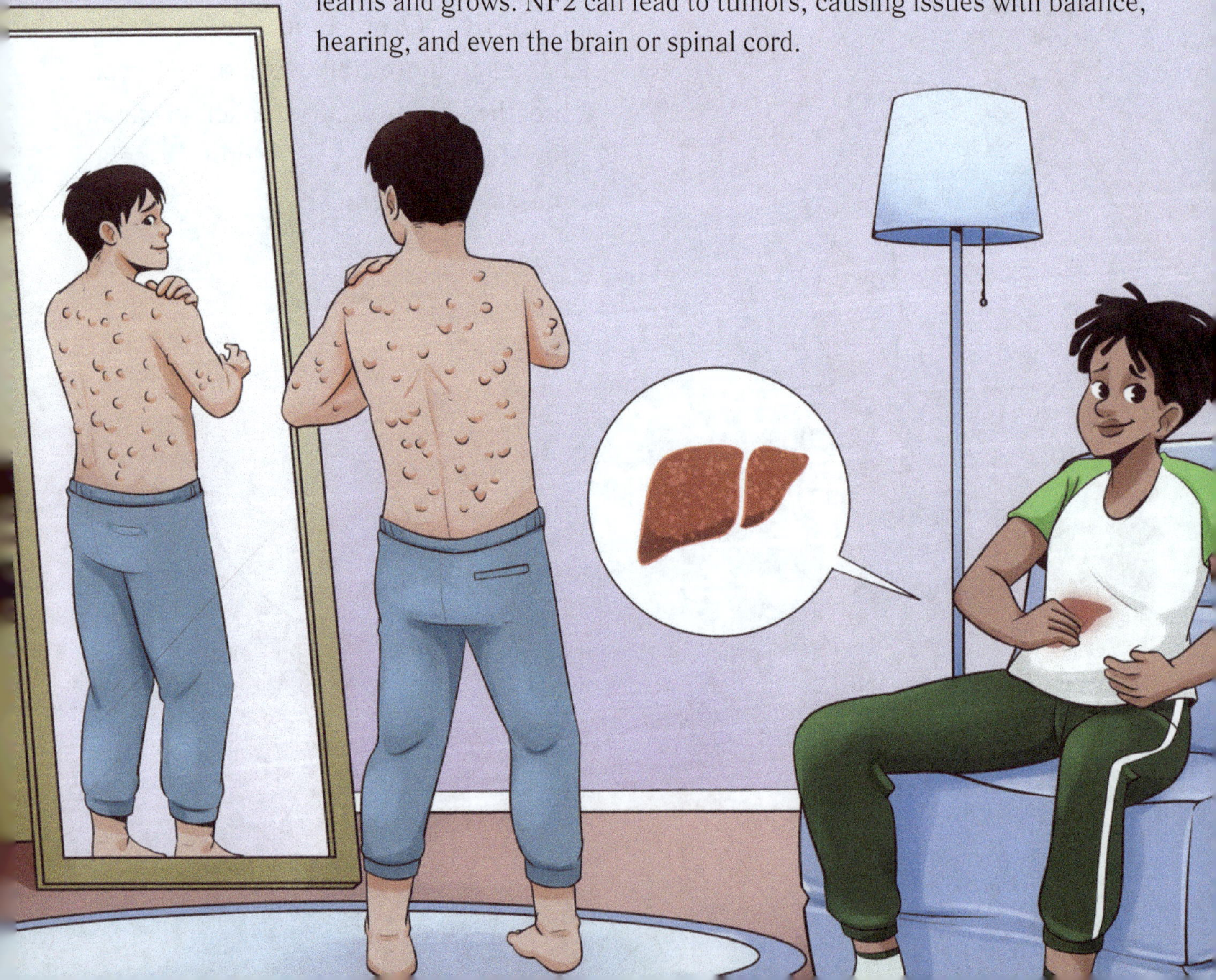

O is for Ogilvie Syndrome and Ollier Disease.

Ogilvie Syndrome is when your colon (large intestine) becomes swollen and doesn't move food properly, even though there is no physical blockage. It's like the muscles in your colon stop working, which can cause pain, bloating, and constipation.

Ollier disease is a rare condition that affects the bones. In this condition, small lumps made of soft, rubbery stuff called cartilage grow inside the bones making the bones grow differently or weaker than normal.

P is for Peripheral Artery Disease, Parkinson's Disease, and Pulmonary Fibrosis.

Peripheral artery disease is a condition where narrowed arteries reduce blood flow to the limbs, usually the legs.

Parkinson's disease is a progressive neurodegenerative disorder that primarily affects movement when part of the brain becomes damaged or dies.

Pulmonary fibrosis is a chronic and progressive lung disease in which lung tissue becomes scarred and stiff over time.

# Q

You are QUICKLY reading this book and learning about rare diseases. Make sure you share this book with a friend. When we all learn about rare diseases, we can make the world a better place.

R is for Rare Skin Disease.

Sometimes, people are born with special kinds of skin that need extra care. These are called rare skin conditions, which just means not many people have them. Some kids might get blisters easily, have really dry skin, or have spots that look different. It's not something you can catch, like a cold—it's just how their skin is.

S is for Sickle Cell Disease and Stargardt Disease.

Sickle cell is a genetic condition that some people are born with. It affects the red blood cells in your body. These cells don't move as easily through the body, and they can get stuck and block blood from flowing. That can cause pain and make someone feel very tired or sick sometimes.

Stargardt disease is a rare inherited retinal condition that can lead to progressive and debilitating vision loss.

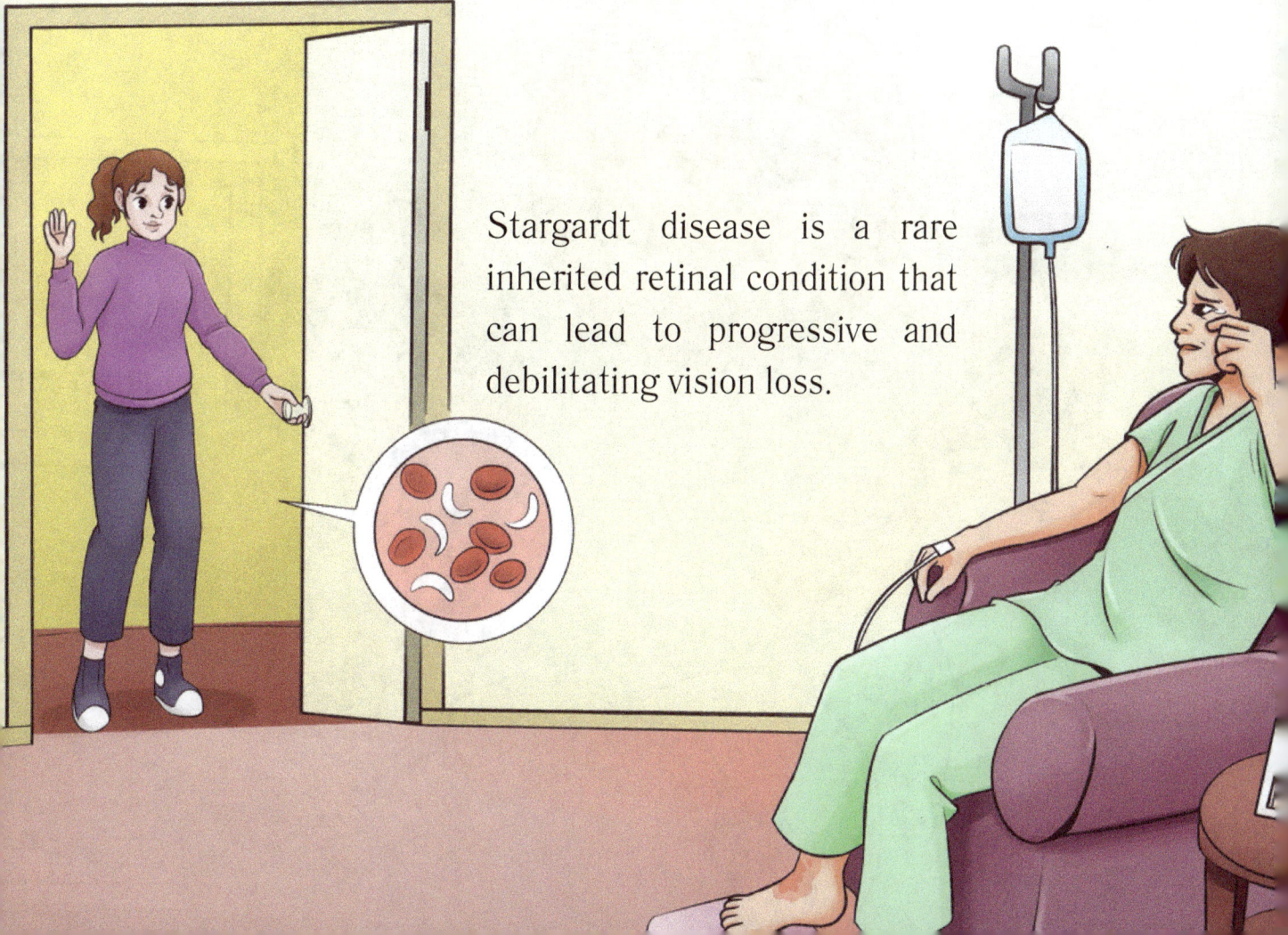

T is for Type 1 and 2 diabetes, and Tangier Disease.

Type 1 diabetes is an autoimmune disease in which the immune system attacks and destroys the insulin-producing beta cells in the pancreas. As a result, the body produces little to no insulin.

Type 2 diabetes is a metabolic disorder in which the body either becomes resistant to insulin or does not produce enough insulin to maintain normal blood sugar levels.

Tangier disease is a rare, inherited disorder characterized by extremely low levels of high-density lipoprotein (HDL) cholesterol in the blood.

U is for Usher's Syndrome.

Usher Syndrome is a rare genetic disorder that causes a combination of hearing loss and progressive vision loss due to retinitis pigments. In some cases, it may also affect balance.

V is for Vasculitis.

Vasculitis is a general term that refers to inflammation of the blood vessels. This inflammation can cause the walls of blood vessels to thicken, weaken, narrow, or scar, which can restrict blood flow and damage organs and tissues.

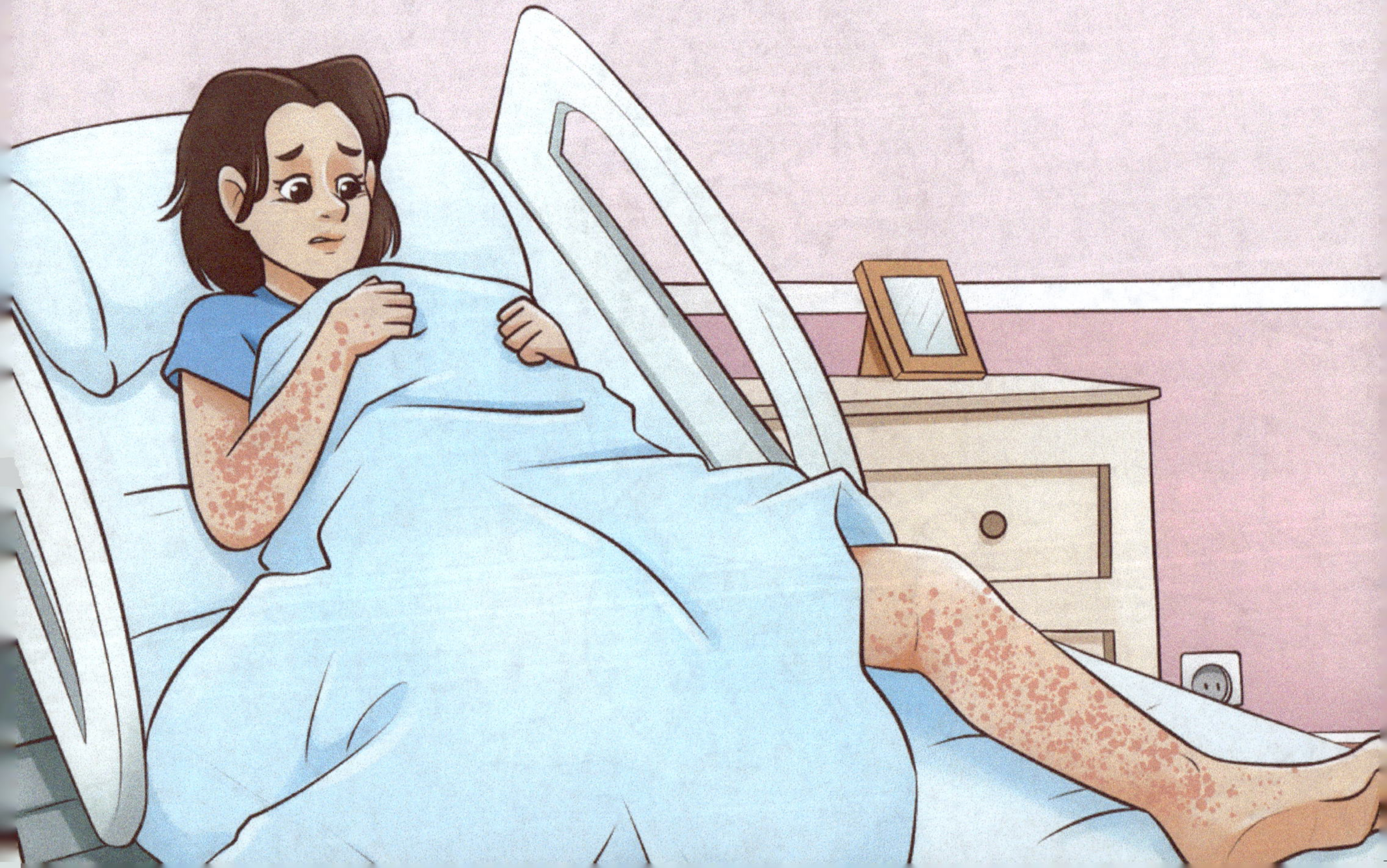

W is for Weaver, Weil, and Werner Syndrome.

Werner Syndrome is a rare, autosomal recessive disorder that causes premature aging in adults.

Werner Syndrome is a rare, inherited disorder that causes rapid aging, usually starting in early adolescence or young adulthood.

Weil Syndrome is a severe sickness that some people and animals can get. It comes from tiny germs that can get into the body and make someone feel very sick.

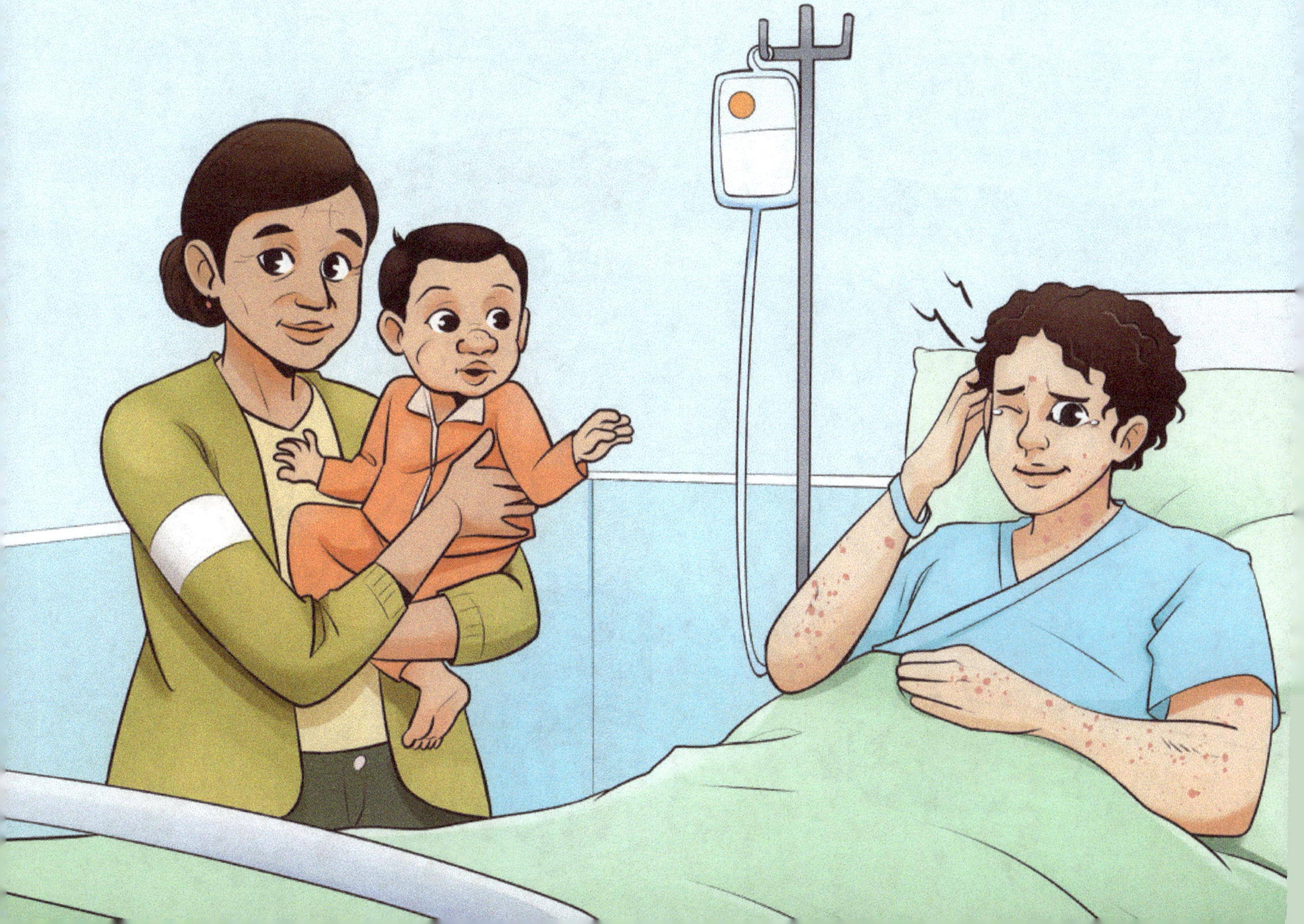

X  is for Xeroderma Pigmentosum.

Xeroderma pigmentosum is a rare, inherited disorder that causes people to be extremely sensitive to ultraviolet light, especially from the sun.

Y is for Yellow Fever and Yunis-Varon Syndrome.

Yellow fever is a severe sickness that people can get from a mosquito bite. It's caused by a virus that can make people feel very sick and even bleed inside their body.

Yunis-Varon Syndrome is a rare genetic disorder present from birth, affecting bone development, facial features, and other body systems.

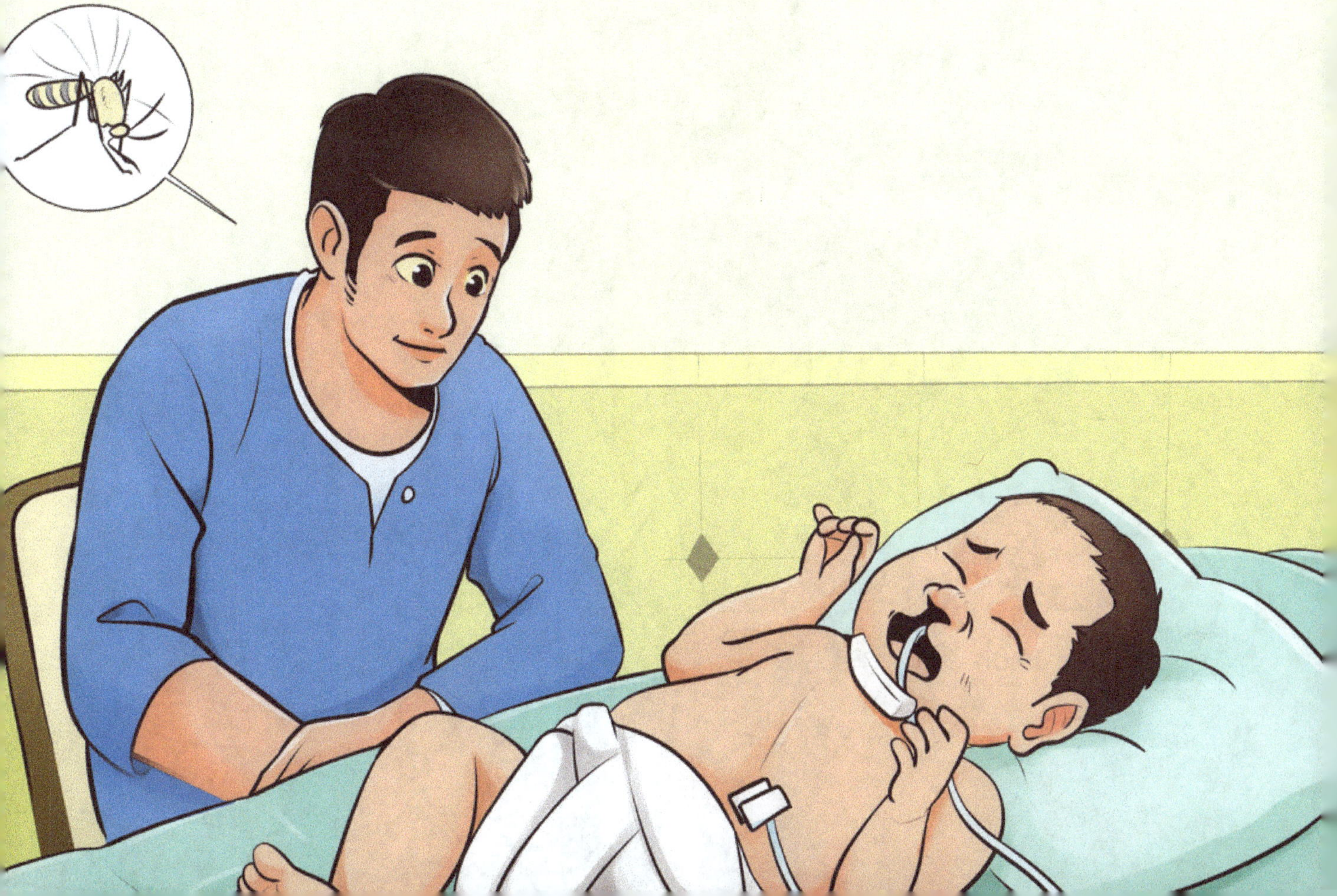

Z is for Zollinger-Ellison Syndrome and Zellweger Syndrome.

Zollinger-Ellison Syndrome is a rare sickness where small lumps called tumors grow in the pancreas or the beginning of the small intestine.

Zellweger Syndrome occurs in babies. It happens when tiny parts inside the body, called peroxisomes, don't work correctly. These parts help keep the body healthy, so when they don't work, the baby can get very sick.

Tumor

There may be more rare diseases that were not mentioned in this book. However, this can be the start of an important conversation. Please share this book with a friend, and let's learn about rare diseases.

www.ingramcontent.com/pod-product-compliance
Lightning Source LLC
Chambersburg PA
CBHW080452100526

44581CB00004B/114